BRITAIN IN OLD PH

LONDON BOROUGH OF BARNET PAST & PRESENT

featuring Arkley, Barnet, Cockfosters, Cricklewood, Edgware, Elstree, Finchley, Friern Barnet, Golders Green, Hadley, Hampstead, Hendon, Mill Hill, New Southgate, Totteridge, Whetstone

PERCY REBOUL &

JOHN HEATHFIELD

SUTTON PUBLISHING LIMITED

Sutton Publishing Limited
Phoenix Mill · Thrupp · Stroud
Gloucestershire · GL5 2BU

First published 1997

British Library Cataloguing in Publication Data
A catalogue record for this book is available from the British Library.

ISBN 0-7509-1378-9

Typeset in 10/12 Perpetua.
Typesetting and origination by
Sutton Publishing Limited.
Printed in Great Britain by
Ebenezer Baylis.

ACKNOWLEDGEMENTS

A book like this is essentially a collaborative effort. The photographs have come largely from out own collections. As always we have been helped by Joanna Corden and Pamela Taylor of the Barnet Borough Archives, and without them the task would probably have been impossible. Liz Holiday was always encouraging and Bill Gelder helped with the proof reading. Our wives have put up with our eccentric interests over many years.

The *Victoria County History* is the starting point for any local historian. Wherever possible original sources have been used, in particular past copies of the local newspapers, available on micro film at Hendon and Barnet libraries.

Author's Note

Wherever possible we have tried to match 'new' and 'old' views by standing where the original photographer stood. This presents many problems, not least of which is that new features often completely obscure the original and roads have often been realigned. It is also impossible in many locations to stand in the middle of a main road, as the original photographer could, without real risk to life and limb!

In some cases the camera angle has been changed where this will reveal additional features of relevance to the story.

CONTENTS

INTRODUCTION

To those living at the beginning of the twentieth century in what is now the London Borough of Barnet it was beyond argument that Britain was the most powerful and prosperous nation on earth. The British Empire which spanned the globe was a prime source of cheap raw materials as well as a market for finished goods made in Britain. The nation's shores were guarded and its overseas possessions policed by a mighty Royal Navy – Britannia ruled the waves in no uncertain terms. The sovereign commanded the love and respect of most of Britain's citizens. The establishment remained largely unchallenged and, for the most part, the teachings of the various churches were accepted without question. Even the irritating Boer War, in which numerous humiliating defeats were suffered, caused hardly a ripple in confidence. Few, if any, could have foreseen the tragedies, traumas and changes that lay ahead.

The people living in the Barnet area, like those in the rest of Britain, knew their place in the world. Class distinction was a matter of utmost concern which affected most aspects of life – dress, manners, education and entertainment to mention but a few. There was very little social mixing of the classes, and a clear distinction between the work of men and women. For the rich few, living in attractive mansions set in acres of gardens, life was extremely comfortable. The middle classes, believing themselves to be (as they still do today) the backbone of the country, could also enjoy many of the comforts that life can offer, helped in no small measure by a ready supply of low-paid servants grateful for the chance of employment of any kind. For the working classes, who formed the bulk of the population, life was often hard and uncompromising, although not without its pleasures. Local jobs were scarce and poorly paid, although the cost of living was low and prices stable. Setbacks such as bad weather, illness or injury, however, could easily result in penury or the dreaded workhouse.

The age, like the half-century that preceded it, was rich in science, technology and invention – electricity, ironclad ships, the motor carriage, telephone and telegraphy, photography – these innovations and many more like them were growing in importance and would soon revolutionize the world. But the most important change had already taken place. The railways had long since established their main lines and many branch lines in the area were in existence by this time. It was now possible to travel with some speed – even daily – in search of work outside the area. Within the next decade, the railways were to be supplemented by the electric-powered tram which offered travel throughout the metropolis at a price most people could afford.

The First World War (1914–18) was a watershed in human affairs. The total economic effort required to win the war showed, among other things, that women could do many of the jobs previously done by men and that their horizons need not necessarily be limited to marriage and the home. They felt, too, that with the coming of peace, their efforts should be recognized by giving them the vote. Full employment and high wages during the conflict also drew workers into factories and away from more traditional (and badly paid) jobs such as farming and domestic service. For many, it was the first time that they had had spare money to spend on 'luxuries' – assuming that such things could be found.

The mid-1920s and '30s, with their economic slumps, brought back the hard times. The political promise to make Britain 'a land fit for heroes' was seen to be another myth. Although jobs remained scarce and wages low, there were changes in the wind that promised better times ahead. Some of these changes were based on new technologies which were developing products such as radios, telephones, motor cars, electrical consumer goods and a host more. The pace of change is revealed in statistics – in 1922, there were nearly a million road licences; by 1930, these had grown to over 2,250,000. Wireless licences in 1923 totalled 595,000; by 1930, the number was over 3,500,000.

The demand for consumer products led, in turn, to the building of factories to make them and the support services to go with them. Areas such as Hendon, Colindale and Chipping Barnet were ideal locations for expansion, particularly when served by new roads such as the North Circular. Most important of all was the need for labour – again reflected in the official figures which show a growth in the London Borough of Barnet population from 76,208 in 1901 to 231,081 in 1931.

Equally significant for the growth of the Barnet area was the political will at national and local level to improve the nation's housing. This included both council houses available at reasonable rents and private housing estates which attracted people of modest incomes wishing to own their home. To support and service the growing population more and better schools were built, new roads laid down, public transport extended and improved and cinemas built to meet the demand for popular entertainment.

The Second World War (1939–45) brought further changes. The years immediately before the war saw large numbers of refugees from mainland Europe settling in areas such as Golders Green, Hendon and Finchley and the need to re-arm Britain brought further prosperity in its wake. During the war itself, with the borough under attack from the air, old class divisions were temporarily laid aside and new social concepts such as 'fair shares for all' accepted by most of the population. Following the war, legislation brought about the National Health Service, a new Education Act and a general move to greater social equality and fairness.

The rebuilding of postwar Europe led to full employment and growing demands for better housing and consumer goods of every description. One of the great changes, affecting everyone, was television which re-started in 1945 following its suspension during the war. It proved to be, temporarily at least, the death knell of established and much-loved leisure activities such as the weekly dance and visit to the cinema, debating societies and sports and social clubs of every description. People began to lose contact with each other. More significantly, television revealed lifestyles which, up to then, could only have been imagined by many viewers. The coming of commercial television brought unprecedented demands for consumer goods that could only be met by a second income and extended credit. The consumer society had arrived – the advent of the 'working wife' was at hand! So, coincidentally, were more effective and available methods of birth control.

The shortages of labour immediately after the war and political upheavals in what had been the British Empire encouraged substantial numbers of emigrants to come to Britain. Other groups such as the Japanese were to come later for different reasons, but the London Borough of Barnet has always been a popular place for immigrants to rebuild their lives and bring up their children. So popular that, as the 1991 census reveals, the London Borough of Barnet has a higher proportion of residents from ethnic groups other than white than Outer London taken as a whole. The excellent race relations in the area is a tribute to all and there is wide acceptance of the richness and diversity of culture brought about by these changes, a striking example being the popularity of ethnic foods.

Of all the products demanded by the fast-growing consumer society to ease drudgery and make life more comfortable, none has been more popular than the motor car. As our photographs show more eloquently than words, the motor car has come to dominate (some would say overwhelm) society. Although its advantages are beyond dispute, the sheer number of vehicles have presented massive social problems such as pollution, death and injury caused by road accidents, traffic jams and even a recently recognized mental condition termed 'road rage'. Successive governments have failed to find an answer. Even the building of new motorways such as the M1 and M25, which bisect the borough, have only served to increase traffic volume by encouraging the building of even more hypermarkets, supermarkets, shopping complexes and industrial buildings of every description. One unfortunate result of this has been the death of many of the High Street shops which served local communities.

As the twentieth century draws to its close, we can see that Britain's role in the world has changed profoundly. The Victorian pillars upon which its greatness was built have disappeared one by one. The country's immense wealth has been dissipated, not least by two world wars; the empire has long since gone and even the royal family, formerly sacrosanct, is subject to bitter criticism and satire. For many people, Britain's only chance of survival and prosperity is as part of a wider European community. Little, in short, remains of those values so dear to our Victorian forebears.

We have, however, been witness to what is probably the most profound change since man peopled the earth. The invention of the microchip, bringing in its wake devices such as the computer and the establishment of a worldwide network of information, represents a quantum leap. But like all great inventions, the benefits are mixed. Job insecurity, we are told, is the major worry of today. Even the traditional 'safe' jobs of yesterday – banking and insurance, for example – are no longer safe. Much of the clerical and routine work previously done by employees is now done by machine resulting in the loss of many thousands of jobs. For others, a new pattern of working from home has evolved in which workers are linked to their businesses by computers and other electronic devices. All of this hints at further variations in the pattern of living in places such as the London Borough of Barnet.

Profound changes are in the air and we can only surmise what people one hundred years hence will think about our own times. Will they, for example, view with disbelief our pollution and exploitation of the earth's resources, or will they regard the twentieth century as some kind of golden age whose quality of life exceeds their own? Time alone will tell.

Percy Reboul, 1997

TOWARDS THE FUTURE . . .

A citizen of the future, eleven-year-old Alistair Delaney working in the computer room of St Mary's School, Finchley.

The Great North Road, Hadley looking north, possibly on Alexandra Rose Day, *c.* 1910. The original road ran north along the west side of Hadley Green, where it can still be traced as a footpath. The road seen here was made by the Whetstone and Highgate Turnpike Trust in about 1740. The road surface and footway have both been metalled. The only traffic on the Great North Road is one cart and one pram. The drinking fountain on the right was erected in 1885.

What was the Great North Road (A1) has retained its name but has been renumbered the A1000. Vandals removed the commemorative plaque on the drinking fountain in the 1980s. There are the inevitable parked cars further along the road.

There has been a brewery at Hadley for over 200 years. In 1887 the original brewery was bought by J. Harris Browne and run as a family business. His rebuilt brewery (1911) is seen here. Water was drawn from artesian wells on the site, which continued to be used as an active brewery until 1938. It was then used as a distribution centre by Fremlins and Whitbreads until 1969.

After being derelict for many years, the Hadley brewery was redeveloped to provide three luxury detached houses built by Newlands Bros Construction Company in the summer of 1996.

Hadley Highstone at the junction with Kitts End Lane and the Great North Road looking south, *c.* 1910. The Highstone marks the spot where the Earl of Warwick is said to have been killed at the Battle of Barnet. It was erected in about 1740 by Sir Jeremy Sambrook of Gobbions, and moved about 100 yards north to its present position about 100 years later. Telephone wires have arrived but as yet no street lights. The Great North Road has been tarmacked but Kitts End Lane is still gravelled. The glasshouses belonged to Warwick Nursery. The Two Brewers Hotel is first mentioned as 'a cottage called the Two Brewers' in 1756.

The nursery was replaced by houses in the 1950s and the Two Brewers burned down in 1990. Efforts have clearly been made to provide houses that blend with the character of what is a conservation area.

High Street, Hadley is now just a continuation of Barnet High Street. This view southward in about 1915 shows Damants Gents Outfitters, Schmidt the Tailor (who made clothes for David Livingstone) and a garage advertising motor repairs. Leafy Victorian suburbia is marked by the trees lining the road.

The buildings themselves have hardly changed in this part of the High Street. 'Portogram' sells high-fidelity audio equipment, while the health food shop sells 'natural' foods not unlike foodstuffs sold in Victorian times. These contrast with the more popular prepacked convenience foods supplied by the supermarkets. Even on a quiet Sunday the High Street is clogged with cars.

The post office and Glebe Lane, Arkley looking east. Before 1914 photographers were rare and nearly everyone in the village has come out to be in the picture. Separate fashions for children are a modern idea and many children are wearing small versions of adult clothes. There is a pile of gravel by the ditch for road mending.

Arkley is relatively unchanged, although the former post office and shop is a private house today. The 30 mph sign is an attempt to reduce traffic speed but is largely ignored by motorists.

Rowley Lane, Arkley looking north. The lane may well follow the line of a Roman track and is typical of most local lanes before the coming of the motor car.

The hedges and trees have matured and street lighting added but otherwise Rowley Lane is unchanged.

The old Bell Inn at Barnet Gate looking east, *c.* 1900. The gate was never a toll gate but was used to prevent cattle straying on to Barnet Common. At this time Bells Cottages were lived in by the Devon family. Note the complete absence of traffic.

The former Bell public house has been renamed The Gate. The Victorian cottages have been cement rendered, but, that apart, the scene is virtually unchanged.

Trent Girls' and Infants' Schools at Cockfosters were the earliest in the district, having been opened in 1838 just before the nearby Christ Church. The first headmistress was Miss Christine Bird. The teacher's house is on the left. Boys attended from the ages of six to nine and girls (for whom the curriculum included 'good plain needlework') from six to twelve.

The old school was pulled down and replaced in 1956 by the one seen here. The architect was K.G. White, church warden and school governor. A further extension was opened in 1959.

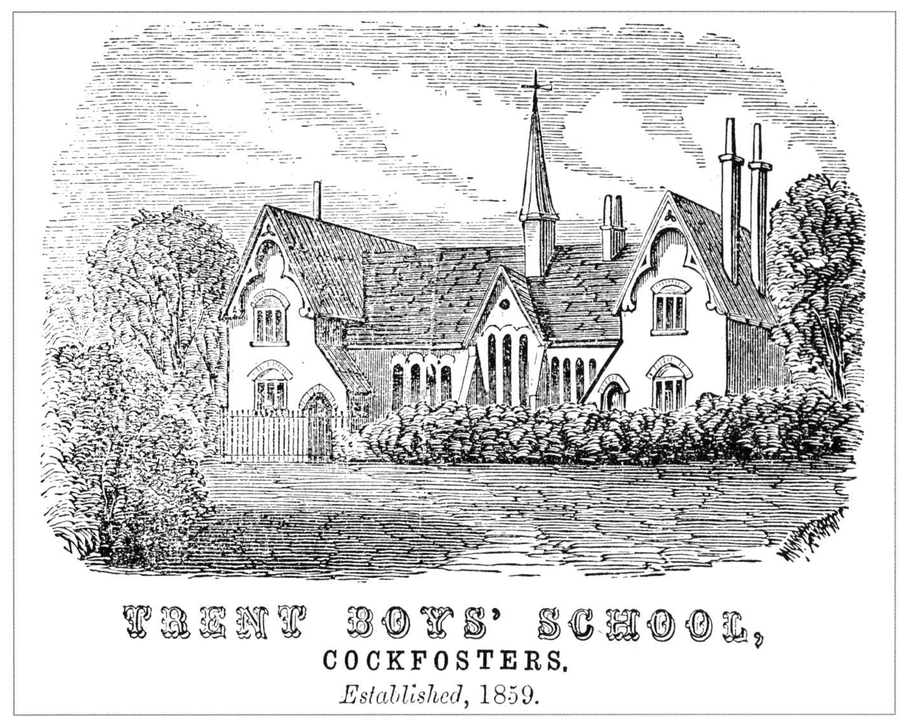

Trent Schools, Cockfosters were on the very edge of the diocese and the borough. The boys' school seen here was probably in Enfield, though the girls' and infants' schools were certainly in Barnet. At the time of opening in 1849 the master was Samuel Etheridge who taught sixty-nine boys assisted by Arthur Forbes, aged sixteen. In 1863, three boys were expelled for smoking (clay pipes at that time). The next day their parents wrote apologies and the following day the boys were readmitted.

The boys' school was closed in 1938 when the boys moved over the road to the other building. The former teacher's house was occupied by the caretaker and the school part became derelict. It was pulled down in the 1970s when part of the site was sold and became a garage. School House is still in private occupation.

Wilson's Cottages, Elstree High Street (which follows the line of a Roman road) looking north, *c.* 1905. Presumably every house with a telephone had its own line. The sailor suit was very popular with boys at that time. The cottages were pulled down in the 1960s.

Westview Gardens, which replaced Wilson's Cottages, were located away from the main road in order to reduce traffic noise. The demand for other houses in a quiet place led to the construction of small 'closes' and cul-de-sacs such as those seen here.

Barnet Barracks, Stapylton Road, *c.* November 1918. The barracks were built in about 1860. The corporal on the left of the front row is 'Curly' Hayes, later caretaker of Queen Elizabeth School for Boys. Sergeant Hyde is on the extreme right with a swagger stick. The 3rd battalion Herts Regt was the training battalion and did not serve abroad. The huts were called 'spiders' for an unknown reason. The site also had married quarters for about twenty families. Part of the brick-built ammunition store is visible on the left.

Barnet Barracks and the adjacent Methodist church were demolished in 1989. The actual barracks site is now a supermarket inside the Spires shopping centre – so-called because the turrets of the church were rather incongruously preserved in the precinct.

Barnet High Street looking west, *c.* 1910. The two boys are wearing Eton collars. The granite sets in the road caused the iron rims of the cart wheels to clatter and ring and there were complaints about traffic noise even then.

Over the years Barnet's largely Victorian shopfronts have been changed or renovated. Typical of such changes is the first shop on the left which is a frozen-food centre with its windows festooned with 'cheap offers'. What was the office of the *Barnet Press*, with the clock on its front wall, is now a bank. The parish church is now shared by Church of England and Non-Conformist congregations.

Church Passage, Barnet, *c.* 1900. The several members of the Baughen family ran a range of local businesses. The 'Boss' always wore a bowler hat as a sign of his status. Mrs Baughen taught at several Barnet schools.

Baughen's is now a Blue Arrow staff agency, but many of the shops went out of business during the economic recession of the 1990s. The latest design of telephone box, which replaced the well-known red variety, accepts plastic cards rather than coins and in so doing discourages thieves.

Barnet Triangle looking south. The standards holding the overhead power cable for the trams are on the side of the road, so the picture dates from just before the First World War. Turning trams round was simple, the driver walked to the opposite end, reversing the seats as he went, and then drove off in the other direction using the alternative driving position. The open staircase at the rear used to frighten at least one local child. The range of traffic is remarkable.

It was impossible to duplicate this view exactly. This part of the High Street was known historically as the 'Squeeze' for obvious reasons. Before the building of the motorways all the traffic along the Great North Road ran through this 14 foot gap. The Kings Head has been on this site since 1626, although it was rebuilt in about 1847. It now competes with the Indian cuisine served next door.

Middle Row, Barnet, *c.* 1885. This is the same site as the previous picture, but viewed from the south. The old market building shown in the centre burned down in 1889. The nearby water cart damped down the dust on the road. At that time the Barnet Gas and Water Company sold water for roads to the council at 1*s* 6*d* (7½ pence) per thousand gallons. Gas lights were erected in Barnet High Road in about 1870.

The site of Middle Row is now a very busy road junction and bus terminus. The Great North Road is now re-numbered as the A1000 following the opening of the Barnet bypass which was designated the A1.

Tudor Hall, Wood Street, Barnet, *c.* 1910. This building housed the Queen Elizabeth School for Boys. The school was founded in about 1573 and moved to a new site in Queens Road in 1932. The headmaster's house is on the right.

The Tudor Hall was partly derelict until 1939 when it was used for civil defence and as a centre to distribute ration books. After the war the site was gradually taken over by Barnet College when the former headmaster's house was demolished.

The blocks in this picture of Barnet Hospital in Wellhouse Lane were built during the First World War to accommodate casualties and consisted of six twenty-bed wards and an operating theatre. The army bell tent in front may have been used by orderlies. The hospital developed out of the workhouse which was built on the site in about 1835.

Barnet Hospital is now part of the Wellhouse Trust. A major rebuilding programme finished in 1997. The entrance block on the right was opened on 23 March 1989 and contains a plaque in memory of Doctor H. Roland Segar, Medical Director from 1925 until 1952 and a notable medical pioneer.

The London and County Bank on the corner of Park Road and the High Road, Barnet, *c.* 1905. The site had previously been Sinclair's grocer's shop. The uniformed groom is waiting in the pony and trap possibly while his employer is in the bank.

The bank is now (since 1967) the National Westminster Bank. The police station, third building further down the hill, was rebuilt in the 1990s.

The junction of Station Road and the Great North Road, Barnet. Station Road was made to connect Barnet with the new station in the green fields about a mile away. Parsloe's bus ran from Arkley to the New Barnet station even after the opening of High Barnet station in 1872.

To accommodate the increase in traffic the junction of High Road and Station Road has been widened and was controlled by traffic lights in 1935. A public lavatory and block of flats replaced Newton's Garage. The service road on the left, which gives access to the shops, is another useful legacy of the 1930s.

Mrs Holmes, wife of the station master at New Barnet station, with one of the Sunday school outings which she used to organize for the children from the St Giles' Mission in London to visit Folly Farm. It was the tradition to decorate the station with flowers.

Electric-powered locomotives, rather than the steam and diesel varieties, now provide the rail service to New Barnet station passengers.

Station Road, New Barnet looking east, *c.* 1925. The ornate town hall seen partially on the left was built on the site of Graffenberg House, described at its sale in 1883 as a 'Hydropathic Establishment'. R.F. Young, the chemist, has his shop on the corner of Lytton Road. The London and South Western Bank dominates the centre of the picture as does the Wesleyan Methodist church on the right.

Both the local Victorian churches, Congregational and Methodist, have been demolished and replaced by a block of flats and office block respectively. The ornate town hall is now an Italian restaurant. The so-called 'wheely bins' in the foreground are a modern method of disposing of household rubbish. Their introduction was widely criticized but they have proved to be more effective than more traditional rubbish bins.

The junction of Station Road and Lytton Road, Barnet looking north, *c.* 1910. E. Fergusson Taylor was in many ways the creator of 'New Barnet' – unjustly forgotten! He was an estate agent and entrepreneur, and lived for a time in the house on the left. He built the New Barnet Assembly Rooms on land hidden behind the large tree. It was here in 1896 that Birt Acres showed moving films for the first time to members of the Lyonsdown Photographic Society.

Belisha beacons such as these in Station Road were introduced in 1935 to lessen the increasing number of road accidents to pedestrians. They were named after the then Minister of Transport, Leslie Hore-Belisha. The chemist's shop has been replaced by an office block (still 'To Let' like many others in the borough) and the seventeen new houses on the left were built by the Metropolitan Housing Association for letting at 'affordable rents'.

Maw's Factory in Cromer Road, Barnet was built in 1921 and closed in 1982. Maw's, established in 1807, were leading makers of surgical supplies and had a large loom making rolls of cotton wool about 6 feet wide. These were then cut down into manageable size. During the Second World War they developed an artificial skin used to treat burns which helped many Battle of Britain pilots.

Maw's Factory was replaced by the Boleyn Way Estate. The imaginative use of trees is a particularly attractive feature of the site.

The police station in Edward Road, Barnet was opened in 1884, closed in 1933 and finally demolished in 1985. There was accommodation at the station for two married officers, eight single men and as many villains as four cells would hold.

After the demolition of the police station the site was scheduled for light industrial use. The Tuning Centre is yet another example of the way in which the motor car dominates the life of late twentieth-century citizens.

Like many others in the immediate neighbourhood, Henry Road, Barnet is named after one of the participants in the Wars of the Roses. The road is marked on the map of 1864, but development was patchy. This photograph dates from about 1926. The car is possibly a BSA or Morgan three wheeler.

Although outwardly unchanged, the Henry Road shops reflect the changes in consumer demand – examples being the motor spares shop and the electrical shop which cater for the do-it-yourself enthusiast. Similarly, the 'World of Pine' meets the current fashion for pinewood furniture.

The foot of Cat Hill, East Barnet looking north with Brookhill Road running along the centre of the picture, *c.* 1920. Early references to Katbrygge date back to about 1553. The Cat public house stood just to the left of the picture.

East Barnet Public Library, on the right, was built in the confident days of the 1960s and '70s when public investment was regarded as a virtue. The shops with living accommodation above date from the same period.

A group of people in their Sunday best gathered for an unknown occasion at Russell's Farm at about the turn of the twentieth century. Russell's Farm in Russell Lane is named after the Russell family, first mentioned in 1325. This pig farm, owned by the Smith sisters in the 1880s, was enlarged as part of the food drive in the First World War.

The 1944 Education Act promised teaching for all according to their age, aptitude and ability and resulted in the introduction of secondary modern schools like that seen here. The building is now part of Barnet College.

The Great Northern Cemetery in what was then Colney Hatch Road was opened in 1861. It had its own railway sidings on the railway line from Kings Cross, where there was a special building for storing coffins. The staff cottages called 'The Retreat' and the chapel seen here stood between the road and the railway. There was a shortage of accommodation in Central London and coffins were often also stored here. The main chapel was in the centre of the cemetery and is still in use.

The Standard Factory, Brunswick Park was opened on this site in 1922. This was land sold by the Cemetery Company. At its peak some 14,000 people were employed here. The first transatlantic speech broadcast was received here on 14/15 January 1923. During the Second World War much military equipment was manufactured here. German flying bombs hit the site in August 1944 resulting in 33 fatal casualties and 212 people being seriously injured.

Whetstone High Road, looking north. The cows belong to the A1 Dairies founded by Mr De Rivaz, a well-respected and well-remembered local employer. The Blue Anchor pub in the background was rebuilt in 1900 and the photograph may well have been taken to commemorate the reopening. This is the Great North Road and the absence of traffic is remarkable.

The Blue Anchor has been replaced by the Mobil petrol station and a DIY block. The cows have been replaced with traffic jams.

Jaques Cottages and Bells Cottages in Whetstone High Road, *c.* 1900. At this time Bells Cottages were owned by Elizabeth Goody. The notice on the cart reads 'Carpets collected and dyed' and refers to the Patent Steam Beating Company on Totteridge Green. John Taylor, the bricklayer, advertises his trade on the wall of his cottage.

Europa House, which replaced Bells Cottages, demonstrates how what was formerly a residential site has become a business property all along the High Road. Many people regret the demolition of old properties with such character, yet few would be prepared to live in the cold and squalor that went with them.

Whetstone Cross Roads looking north, *c.* 1905. The post office on the right was run for over 100 years by the Gilmour family. The Griffin Inn is first mentioned in 1694.

The Himalaya Restaurant reflects the changing nature of our multi-cultural society. Traffic lights were erected here in about 1935 on the site of the old toll gate. The Griffin was rebuilt in 1929 and in 1996 there was a battle to prevent its being called Scruffy Murphy's. The old post office, for thirty-nine years occupied by Studio Cole, has been refurbished and opened in 1996 as a pizza parlour.

The junction of Whetstone High Road and Totteridge Lane looking north, *c.* 1875. There has been a baker's shop on this corner since before 1819. An early gas lamp can be seen in Totteridge Lane.

After more than a century the Harper family gave up their businesses, but the tradition of hand baking on the premises has continued. The buildings seen here are scheduled for demolition.

No. 19 Oakleigh Park North, *c.* 1900. The estate was sold in 1867 and development had begun by 1871. This house was used as Oakleigh Park Prep School for many years. In 1939 it housed an Auxiliary Fire Service unit.

Because the houses in Oakleigh Park have large gardens they are a target for developers, who thereby provide homes for many on land previously occupied by few. Here at least an effort has been made to provide an attractive design in keeping with the style of the district.

All Saints' Church, Myddleton Park is considered by many to be the centre of Whetstone, though it is in the parish of Friern Barnet. Built in 1881 by John Miles, the first vicar was his son Henry Miles.

All Saints' Vicarage was demolished to make way for Cameron Close. Ward Griswold Cameron was born in Montreal, Canada on 13 April 1889. On 23 January 1933 he became the second vicar of All Saints' Church.

Gallants Farm in Russell Lane, seen here, seems to be of Tudor origin. The Russell family owned land nearby some 500 years ago. This was essentially a dairy farm, although what appear to be sheep are mowing the lawn.

Beresford and Wierdale Avenues occupy the site of the old farm house. Part of the Gallants Farm estate was sold on 22 February 1934. The 49 acres went for about a pound each to the Ideal Homes Company.

The Hand and Flower in Whetstone High Road, *c.* 1865. The man in the picture is thought to be Robert Gilmour, post master and the last keeper of the Whetstone toll gate. Elm trees said to have been planted by Richard Attfield were a feature of the High Road.

The Hand and Flower was demolished in 1987. It was replaced by Barclays Bank. The small wooden hut (by the parked van) housed, in 1904, the Whetstone fire station, equipped with 400 feet of hose, a manual pump and various tools. The Whetstone Fire Brigade consisted at that time of five part-time volunteers led by Mr Howard, a local builder. The hut was last used by the fire brigade in 1920. The hut was then taken over by TocH. The large office building to the right is now used by VAT Watkins. A lone tree is struggling to survive the traffic pollution.

The junction of Friern Barnet Lane and the Great North Road, *c.* 1890. The road makers have left a pile of gravel for future use. Three generations of Cooks ran the baker's shop on the corner with the cart outside.

The Three Horseshoes' exterior has hardly changed in over 100 years. The police station in Friern Barnet Lane replaced the earlier (1861) station in the High Road. It was built on the site of Floyd's dairy farm.

Whetstone High Road near the junction with Rasper Road looking north, *c.* 1907. Whetstone Place is on the left. The Swan with Two Necks pub can be seen beyond the terrace.

Whetstone Place was burned down in May 1939 in order to provide practice for the local civil defence units which were preparing for the Second World War. Swan Court, which replaced it, is typical of the postwar council building. The Swan with Two Necks further north has been replaced by two blocks of flats, North and South Place. The introduction of central heating means that the flats have no chimneys.

Newton's bicycle shop was at 8 St John's Terrace, Whetstone opposite the church. The whole family have come out to be in the picture. Cycling was a very popular pastime at the turn of the century. As the business improved Newton's eventually ran a garage in Barnet.

There is no cycle shop left in Whetstone now. Angelo's fast-food shop with its vibrant, remodelled front reflects today's fashion for convenience food.

Poynter's Grove, Totteridge Green was built in about 1780 and was lived in for nearly 100 years by the Puget family, who were very generous in the district. Geraldine Harmsworth, mother of the newspaper magnate Lord Northcliffe, lived there after 1896. The grounds were said to have been laid out by Capability Brown. The trees are part of a formal drive running south across Totteridge Green.

Poynter's Grove was demolished in about 1938. The present houses were commandeered by the military in 1939 and used as officers' quarters.

The Orange Tree Hotel and Tea Gardens is mentioned in the War Office billeting return of 1756, when it had stabling for two horses. Frank Collis was proprietor in about 1920. This was a popular meeting place for the many cycling clubs active at the turn of the century.

The Orange Tree remains a popular venue for drinkers of all ages. Like much of Totteridge, it has changed little over the years.

Totteridge village post office and general shop also served teas on Sunday afternoons. In 1893 the post master was George Keynes. The road surface is of rolled gravel and the only traffic appears to be a few chickens at the edge of the road.

Thanks to the vigilance and efforts of the Totteridge Preservation Society and others, the essential character of the village has remained intact.

The eighteenth-century Priory House on the right served as the Urban District Council offices from 1906 onwards. The Orange Tree pub on the left was originally built in Tudor times and rebuilt in about 1923. Legend has it (and it may well be true) that Queen Elizabeth I took refreshments at the inn on her journey from Hatfield House to London when she became queen.

The distinctive lines of the Friern Barnet town hall can be seen on the right. It opened in 1940, during the war, and was the headquarters of civil defence. The bus terminus located on the forecourt carries passengers to the West End and beyond. The Orange Tree pub, in keeping with a fashionable trend by brewery marketing people, has been renamed Big Hand Mo's.

Smith's Cottages in Colney Hatch Lane were owned by George Knight Smith, an important local benefactor. Mr Paul, an early film maker, who specialized in exciting fire scenes, used the nearby Orange Tree as his headquarters. In 1909 these cottages were accidentally burned down during the making of a film.

Following the fire, the Hollyfield Estate, comprising part of Hillside Farm, was laid out for building in 1903 by E.C. Day to form St John's and Hollyfield Roads. The shops were built in the 1930s, as were the houses down the hill. The highway, an ancient one, remains an important traffic route to and from central London.

St Michael's was founded in 1896 in an iron hut on the Brunswick Park Estate. The red-brick church was built in 1902 at a cost of £5,000. The church hall was added in 1913. The *Barnet Press* for 2 November 1880 reports the Brunswick Park Estate being laid out in 200 building plots, on land sold by the Great Northern Cemetery Company.

The church was pulled down in 1973 and the site cleared in 1977. In 1972 the parish of St Michael's South Barnet was incorporated into the four neighbouring parishes. The land was transferred to the Church Commissioners for housing.

Corn harvesting at Hollickwood. The corn is being bound into sheaves which are then stooked to dry out before being threshed. The Hollickwood is mentioned in 1623 and a hatch gate into Friern Barnet Lane existed in 1810. In 1846, 61 acres were sold and eventually became part of Colney Hatch Hospital.

Following the closure of Friern Hospital, development of some of the land commenced. The fields and meadows in this part have been completely built over with modern multi-storey flats and houses.

St John's Church in Friern Barnet Road was designed by J.L. Pearson at the request of the Revd Frederick Hall, the first vicar, and built in 1891. Hall asked Pearson to base his design on a medieval church near the River Rhine. As a result St John's includes some of the most flamboyant flying buttresses ever designed by a Victorian architect, although these are not properly visible from the road. Macdonald Road, here built up on one side only, was laid out in 1887 by the London Land Company.

A notable addition to the scene is the Friern Barnet Public Library built in 1933/4. The service road alongside the library has set aside a parking place for disabled drivers. This reflects increasing awareness in recent times of the special needs of such people, although much remains to be done. The church is largely unchanged.

Friern Barnet Road before the trams came in 1909. The lines down the centre of the road were made by cart wheels. The cast-iron railings in front of the houses are of good design and typify suburban villa taste of the period.

Today high-speed drivers have to be deterred from killing each other by painting white lines in the centre of the road (to prohibit overtaking) and the provision of traffic islands.

Colney Hatch Asylum for the Lunatic Poor was opened in July 1851. The ornate Italianate façade is the work of Samuel Dawkes. The whole building cost over £300,000, which, at the prices of the day, made it the most expensive hospital built up to that time. From the start the medical practice was based on light, hope and kindness. Throughout its history it was at the forefront of psychiatric treatment.

With more enlightened attitudes to the welfare and treatment of the mentally sick, the role of the hospital changed in postwar years. Renamed Friern Hospital, it was finally declared redundant in the 1990s and became a prime target for development. Work continues on the site to build a retail park, restaurant and more houses with the famous front being turned into luxury flats. These are scheduled for completion in March 1998 and will be followed by further development work.

New Southgate railway bridge, *c.* 1909. Although the tram lines have been laid, there appear to be no standards for the overhead power cables. As with so many other parts of the borough, it was the coming of the railway that provided the stimulus for house building.

Buses, cars and commercial vehicles of every description and weight now cross the railway bridge which once saw trams and trolleybuses on their way to Wood Green. The former Railway Tavern on the left has been renamed The Turrets.

The entrance to Frenchman's Farm in Friern Barnet Lane near St James' churchyard, *c.* 1895. The Frenchman was Pierre Baume (1797–1875), who bought the farm in 1852. Gas mains belonging to the Colney Hatch Gas, Light and Coke Company had been laid along here as early as 1867. A gas lamp can be seen in the background.

Frenchman's Farm was sold at the turn of the twentieth century and good quality houses built on part of the land from 1910 onwards. Bethune Park and its nine-hole golf course were built by the local council in about 1926 on another part of the land. The Queen's Well is marked by a stone column on the left and to the right is the boundary fence of St James' Parish Church.

NEW SOUTHGATE

New Southgate railway station was originally called Colney Hatch and served the asylum. In order to spare the embarrassment of local residents, the name was changed to New Southgate. The platforms were enlarged in 1890. There are coal trucks in the sidings. Local coal merchants included Charringtons, Herbert Clarke and the Co-op.

Steam and diesel traction have been replaced by electric motors powered by overhead cables. The coal sidings have gone, reflecting the clean air legislation of the 1950s and the demise of the British coal industry. Graffiti, a puzzling form of vandalism, has grown to epidemic proportions and, as on the platform seat, defaces most public buildings and public transport.

The name The Priory was given to several large houses in this district in Victorian times. This one stood at the junction of Friern Barnet Road and Bowes Road, New Southgate. It is a splendid example of Victorian Gothic and dates from about 1855.

Charles Holder's award-winning station at nearby Arnos Grove (1932/3) was a stimulus to substantial redevelopment, two generations of which are pictured here. Many would say that the more modern building on the right shows a lamentable decline in standards of design.

Station Road, New Southgate looking north before the arrival of the trams. The nearby estate was designed to the highest standards of the day and many successful businessmen lived there. Easy access to the City via the railway was a good selling point. Land was sold by G.K. Smith to the United Estates and Investment Company in 1890. The shops were an important amenity when so many people had to walk everywhere.

The shops were demolished in the 1950s and replaced by a four-storey block of flats. There is a bus shelter just north of the pedestrian crossing.

The McCurd lorry factory in Finchley High Road at the junction with Woodside Grove was built during the First World War and made lorries and repaired engines. By the 1920s the factory was used by the De Dion Company, specialists in making high quality rear axles.

The site's involvement with vehicles has been preserved with the Kwik Fit depot devoted to the replacement of vehicle exhaust systems and tyres. It provides a 'do-it-while-you-wait' service to customers.

The skating rink in North Finchley High Road opened in 1910. At that time there were uniformed instructors and a string orchestra for an early form of aerobics. Skating did not create enough profit, so the rink became a cinema in 1912.

The Rink Cinema was replaced by the transport company Carrimore Six Wheelers in 1923. It then became a Metropolitan Police depot in 1970, which was itself closed in 1997.

Tally Ho Corner, Finchley is named after the 'Tally Ho' stage coach owned by the Chaplin family in the 1820s. The coach ran from London to Birmingham and the first change of horses was at Chaplin's Finchley stables, called therefore Tally Ho stables. This view looking north dates from about 1900, before the trams came through in 1905. Prior's department store, family owned, was relocated to the corner of Castle Road in the 1930s. The newly planted trees are a sign of the civic pride felt by the new community created by the coming of the railway in 1872.

Even in quiet times, Tally Ho Corner is clogged with traffic. Advertising columns such as the one seen here are a recent development – the subject of fierce public opposition.

Tally Ho Corner looking south. Type 'A' tram number 121 is on its way to Highgate. Other trams ran to Golders Green along Ballards Lane on the right. The junction where the tram lines crossed was a traffic hazard. Tram lines were also likely to trap the wheels of bicycles. The Park Road Hotel is to the right of the picture. Alfred Baker's watchmakers shop is on the left.

The hotel was renamed The Tally Ho! in 1927. The small plot of land in front of the pub, which once housed public lavatories, now features a telephone kiosk and a small garden with shrubs and seats. The seat, like so many others in the borough, has been vandalized.

The Cricketers, North Finchley (with adjacent cottages) was a Victorian pub standing at the original junction of Nether Street and the High Road. The road layout was altered in 1935.

Although the original Cricketers pub is structurally unchanged and there is no evidence that stage coaches (or any other coaches) ever stopped there, its name has been changed to The Coach Stop. The Victorian cottages have been replaced by shops – one of them a betting shop which is a reminder that street betting was illegal a century ago.

The Kingsway, Finchley was laid out in 1933 to improve access from Woodhouse Road to the tram depot in Woodberry Grove. The new road ran through the grounds of Orchard Lodge, owned by T.C. Newman, a prominent local benefactor.

The triangle of land bounded by Nether Street, High Road and Kingsway, has had a chequered career. It once housed the Gaumont Cinema, opened in 1937 and demolished in 1987. The empty site now houses a market. The bus terminus, which in the 1930s and '40s handled trolleybuses, still survives. There are currently ambitious plans for redevelopment in which Finchley citizens are hoping for some kind of cultural/art centre.

The junction of Ballards Lane and Nether Street, Finchley, probably just before the tram lines were laid, *c*. 1905. Nether Street continues on the right. The parade of shops on the left displays a high degree of luxury in the decoration and contrasts strongly with Jelks' furniture warehouse and the older shops on the right. The footpath has been paved, but the road surface still appears to be rolled gravel.

There has been a chemist's shop on the corner of Ballards Lane and Nether Street since the row of shops was built at about the beginning of the twentieth century. Some of the attractive original pargetting on the gables of the shops still survives. The coming of two large supermarkets in the immediate area has created severe competition for the smaller local traders.

Ballards Lane, Finchley is probably named after the Ballard family, local landowners at the beginning of the fourteenth century. Princes Parade stood at the junction with Long Lane. There are two horsebuses heading in opposite directions and a pony and trap.

The Ballards Lane–Long Lane intersection remains a busy location where, at most times of the day, a queue of vehicles will be seen negotiating the dangerous junction. The large number of ethnic food shops is a feature of today's Parade.

Pope's Garage in Ballards Lane was one of the earliest in the district. Among other things, they made the motorized sledges used on Scott's Antarctic expedition. Popes' Alley ran west next to the garage.

It is a rare event to see a building devoted to the requirements of the motorist demolished and replaced by something else – in this case Tesco's supermarket which caters for another overwhelming human passion, food and drink. Part of the wide appeal of such shops is their provision of a car park which removes the fear of street parking fines.

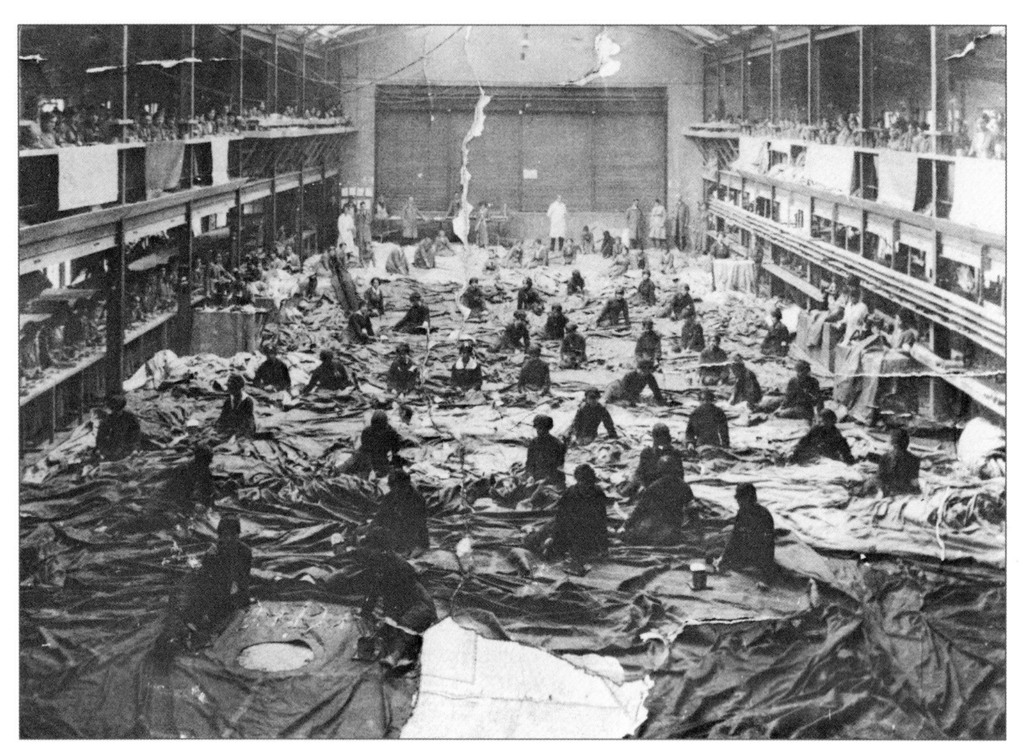

Observation balloon making at the old Bohemia Cinema in Ballards Lane during the First World War. This cinema replaced an earlier one at the Wentworth Hall, and was itself replaced by the New Bohemia at 328 Ballards Lane.

The Old Bohemia building was situated between Princes and Redbourne Avenues. After use for many years as a factory, it was demolished in the 1990s and replaced by a small housing estate. This view is taken through the iron-bar gates located in the High Road, possibly the only surviving feature from earlier days.

Church End station, Finchley. The railway was built in 1872 as an extension of the line from Moorgate through Finsbury Park to East Finchley. A northbound train waits at the platform. The refreshment kiosk advertises beers and wines. Finchley power station, in Squires Lane, owned by the local council, can be seen in the distance.

Finchley Central station, today part of the Northern Line underground system, was electrified in 1940. Some elements of the Victorian station still survive, notably the footbridge and the 'dogtooth' decoration, although both these features have been restored.

The junction of Hendon Lane and Regents Park Road, Finchley, *c.* 1910. St Mary's School is on the right with the Manor Farm dairy shop on the corner of Victoria Avenue. Clement's Nursery is in the centre of the junction. A tradesman is watering his horse at one of the many drinking troughs provided by the Metropolitan Drinking Trough Association. Christ's College is visible in the background.

A much changed location. The nursery was replaced in 1911 by King Edward's Hall which, among other things, served as a hospital during the First World War. St Mary's School was closed in April 1990 and relocated at Dollis Park N3. Subsequently the County Court was built on the site, an attractive building enhanced by some of the original trees.

Finchley fire station in Royal Terrace on the north-west side of Hendon Lane was in the middle of a row of shops. The crew was a mixture of full and part-time firefighters. The first superintendent was George Pope. Between 1900 and 1905 the men fought an average of fourteen fires per year.

The fire station was later to occupy more of the shops, but moved to a purpose-built site at the junction of Long Lane/North Circular Road in about 1930. The shops still survive – many of them dedicated to the pursuit of youth and beauty and the illusions that go with them.

Avenue House in East End Road, Finchley was built by Plowmans for Edward Cooper in about 1858 and bought by H.C. Stephens in about 1878. He was owner of the famous ink company and known as the uncrowned king of Finchley. At his death in 1918 he left the house and gardens to Finchley Council. During the First World War the house was used as a convalescent home for the Royal Flying Corps.

Avenue House still stands today. A disastrous fire in 1989 badly damaged parts of the building but these have been sympathetically restored. The building is 'home' to many local groups and charities including the Finchley Society whose work to preserve the history of Finchley has included the foundation and maintenance of the Stephens Collection in the museum room of Avenue House and The Friends of Avenue House Grounds.

The Old Five Bells in East End Road, Finchley, with an attractive pleasure garden, can just be seen on the left. The billeting return of 1756 shows The Bell as having one room and no stables. Gas street lighting was introduced here in about 1885.

Although the pub retains some of its rural charm, the intrusive, colourful signs are a reminder of the importance of 'passing trade' to modern retailing.

The market-place, East Finchley looking south. This was originally a hog market, founded on land just west of the Great North Road by the Odell family who opened the nearby George Inn in about 1780. They had previously been hog farmers near Totteridge Lane. Finchley became one of the country's largest hog markets. Nearly everyone in the photograph is wearing a hat.

In addition to its deplorable sanitary conditions and general decay, the market-place suffered badly in air raids during the Second World War. Redeveloped in the 1960s, little survives of its original character. The entrance to Holy Trinity School can be seen on the right.

East Finchley railway station was opened in 1867 as part of the Great Northern Railway. Grays the coal merchants used their office there for over forty years. The tram standards are in the centre of the road. They were a traffic hazard and were moved to the sides of the roads in about 1912.

Today's East Finchley station replaced the original version in about 1939, when the line was electrified and became part of the Barnet branch of the Northern Line underground. It is a good example of late 1930s' railway architecture and notable for the Jacob Epstein sculpture of an archer which can just be seen atop the building. The sculpture, which faces south, celebrates the building of the 17½-mile tunnel which links East Finchley and Morden at the other end of the line.

Fortis Green Road at the junction with Eastern Road looking west. This estate was largely laid out by W. Collins who lived in Fortismere, a grand house near the Muswell Hill end of the road. Located on a gravel ridge, Fortis Green was a highly desirable place to live and many of the houses have considerable architectural merit.

Many of the fine houses in Fortis Green have survived and it remains an attractive though very busy thoroughfare.

East Finchley High Road looking north near Falkland Avenue. The Congregational chapel on the corner of East End Road was enlarged in 1846. This was a rapidly developing area built after the coming of the railway. All goods that came in on the railway were delivered by horse and cart. The railways operated passenger trains by day and goods trains at night.

This stretch of the High Road is particularly busy. The Congregational chapel was demolished in 1965 to make way for a supermarket although The Bald Faced Stag on the corner of East End Road still survives. The pavement shown here is typical of those used today in which smaller slabs of artificial stone are interlarded with bricks – a contrast with the uniformity of the previous larger slabs of artificial stone used to surface pavements.

Finchley Cottage Hospital was first talked about as part of the celebrations for Queen Victoria's Jubilee in 1897. Although backed by Ebenezer Holman, a prominent Finchley citizen, fund raising was slow and the hospital did not open until 1908. Further funds were raised to commemorate the First World War and in 1922 the name was changed to Finchley Memorial Hospital.

The hospital did sterling service in the Second World War and with its facilities added to from time to time continues to serve the area.

Finchley Garden Village off Lyndhurst Gardens, *c.* 1930. Raising funds for Finchley Memorial Hospital was always difficult. Finchley Carnival was started to help and in its wake came many sports days and other events like that seen here.

The village green remains and the houses are unchanged. The community spirit, while perhaps not as strong as in earlier days, is still a feature.

Finchley open-air swimming pool was opened in 1933 and was an immense success. Weekly attendance figures of over 13,000 were reported in the *Finchley Press*. So many people attended that time was rationed by the use of coloured arm bands issued at set periods.

The original swimming pool was replaced in the 1990s by a large complex of sports and entertainment facilities including a golf driving range, an indoor swimming pool, fitness centre and cinemas. The development was controversial, not least because it required further tranches of land from the Roughlots, which survived from the old Finchley Common.

Hendon Central underground railway station, *c.* 1923. The Underground Electric Railway Company's extension of the track from Golders Green to Edgware was delayed by the First World War. Hendon Central station, built by Carmichael's of Wandsworth to designs by the company's engineers, soon provided a stimulus to house building.

Hendon Central station, with added storeys and shops and maisonettes abutting each end, faces a six-line highway with a metal fence down its centre to prevent jay-walkers crossing the busy road. Underpasses have been built to encourage safe crossing. The original roundabout has gone with traffic now controlled by traffic lights. The bus stop, which originally stood in front of the station, is now located 100 metres to the north.

The Burroughs, Hendon, *c.* 1900. The Burroughs is named after the hill on which it stands and is first mentioned in 1316. The low white buildings on the right were the parish cottages (almshouses really) with the old parish workhouse behind them.

The pathetic remnant of the borough's pond incorporates a non-working fountain and underpasses for pedestrians to cross the busy carriageways. The Georgian houses on the left have survived but the original cottages on the right were replaced by the Quadrant Close block of flats in 1934.

Parsons Street, Hendon, *c.* 1910. Metal plates bearing the names of roads had recently been introduced. Carter's Garage replaced an earlier livery stables and coach builder's yard. In her will of 1758, Elizabeth Parsons left an income of £100 to the poor of the parish.

Little remains of the rural character of Parsons Street. The area on the right was developed in the 1930s with the Quadrant Parade terrace of shops and maisonettes. The other side retains some of its original houses and a notable survival is Hammond's vehicle-repair business which opened in 1928. The horse chestnut tree in the centre is possibly a survivor from the original trees which lined the road.

Bell Lane, Hendon, *c.* 1922. A brewer's lorry is being unloaded outside the pub. The hoardings are advertising Charles Hawtrey appearing at the Criterion Theatre, Bovril, Maggi soups and Veritas. Wilby's undertakers shop can just be seen on the right.

Although the Bell Lane–Brent Street junction is still recognizable, much has changed. The bus terminus no longer exists; the public lavatories have been replaced by a single stainless steel 'facility' regarded with suspicion and distrust by most citizens and the buildings on either side of The Bell were demolished in the 1970s to make way for the Sentinel Square development.

Hendon railway station was opened for passengers by the London, Midland and Scottish railway in 1868. There was a separate station for the nearby Welsh Harp Pleasure Grounds. There are three delivery carts standing outside the shops on the right, another reminder of the importance of the horse.

The road bridge over the M1 motorway has replaced the former shopping parade. The Railway Hotel, now called The Hungry Horse, is all that remains.

The bridge in Finchley Lane over the Dollis Brook which marks the boundary at that point between Hendon and Finchley. The weirs are marked on the 1896 map.

The bridge today carries Hendon Lane traffic to and across the busy A1 road. The land on the north side of the Brent was for many years a garden centre but was sold in the late 1990s for housing. Note the double-garage door on the left. Most families in this prosperous part of the borough own at least two cars.

Greyhound Hill, Hendon, with Vine Cottages on the left was called Hall Lane until about 1915. The hill is named after The Greyhound pub. This was originally called Church House because the rents were used by the church to help the poor of the parish. It was also used for vestry meetings. The first reference to The Greyhound is in 1655, but the site was probably developed before then. Hinges Model Dairy Farm is on the left with Church Farm opposite.

The forecourt of The Greyhound can still be seen but Vine Cottages, said to be Hendon's oldest buildings, were demolished in 1935. A small public garden with seating has taken their place.

Cool Oak Lane, also called Cool Duck Lane, looking east, *c.* 1910. The Welsh Harp reservoir was created by damming the River Brent near its junction with the Silk Stream in order to provide water to the Grand Union Canal. The buildings of the Welsh Harp Pleasure Grounds can be seen on the right and Stanley Road on the left.

Cool Oak Lane, which runs parallel to the busy North Circular Road, is used as a so-called 'rat run' by many motorists. Activities on the Welsh Harp Pleasure Grounds, like so much else, were badly affected with the coming of television although it is still widely used by boating and bird-watching enthusiasts. The buildings on the left are the headquarters of the Welsh Harp Youth Sailing Centre.

Hendon postmen's office probably shortly after its opening in about 1913. The range of headgear reflects the differing status of the employees. Sorters wore an indoor uniform as they did not deliver letters.

Hendon post office, with a large sorting office at the rear, was built in 1939 to accommodate the vast increase in demand for postal services from a growing population.

The Rose and Crown, Brent Street, Hendon. Brent Street runs on down to the River Brent. The boys appear to be wearing sailor collars so the picture may well date from about 1905.

Very little remains today of the earlier Brent Street. Among the major changes was the addition of the Sentinel Square shopping precinct on the right built in the 1970s. It required a substantial amount of demolition of old buildings and has changed the whole character of the area. Traffic problems are horrendous in spite of the construction of lay-bys such as that seen here on the left.

Hendon Aerodrome developed from a group of buildings in a field bought by Claude Graham White in 1910. It rapidly became one of the country's leading flying schools. After a nasty dispute with the Treasury, the aerodrome was taken over by the RAF in 1922. Regular flying displays were a popular attraction in the 1920s and '30s, here featuring what seems to be an Avro 504.

The last RAF pageant was in 1937 and the aerodrome closed to flying in 1957 when much of the land was used to build the Graham Park housing estate. The aviation tradition has happily not been lost entirely. In 1973 part of the land was used to build the RAF Museum, one of the finest museums of its kind in the world.

Holders Hill, Hendon, sometimes called Olders Hill. The straw boaters suggest this photograph was taken at the turn of the twentieth century.

Most of the fine Victorian houses in Holders Hill were replaced with blocks of flats in the 1950s and '60s. Fortunately, a number of the trees have survived.

Church Road, Hendon at the junction with Parsons Street. Cook and Sons builders of 1 Parsons Street were established in 1869. This junction was often called Cooks Corner.

A much changed Cooks Corner and Church Road. A complex of arcaded sheltered homes for the elderly was built in the 1990s to replace the ill-fated Odeon Cinema, which opened a few weeks before the outbreak of the Second World War in September 1939. A number of the original shops and flats still survive on the eastern side of Church Road.

Church Farmhouse, Hendon, *c.* 1900. The farmhouse dates from the mid-seventeenth century. When this picture was taken the farm was run by the Dunlop family, and produced, like many other farms in the area, hay for the London market and dairy cattle.

Church Farm was fortunate to survive political pressure to have it demolished and became a museum in 1955. Its lively, imaginative and varied exhibition programmes add much to the cultural life of the borough.

The Broadway, West Hendon shortly after the tram standards were moved to the sides of the roads, *c.* 1913. Passengers are standing in the middle of the road to board the tram. The Express Dairy on the left was so called because the milk came up to London on special express trains often called the milk train.

Considering the important location of the Broadway, remarkably little has changed. Trams have been replaced by buses, gas light by electricity and cars dominate the scene. The numerous 'To Let' signs may indicate a slackness in trade although they can also be an early warning of a site ripe for replacement.

Golders Green station, probably soon after the line opened in 1907. At that time the branch of what is now the Northern Line was called the Hampstead Tube. The bus has three horses.

Golders Green station has become a major terminus for travellers, its forecourt used both by local buses and long-distance coaches. An adjacent taxi rank is also much used. The nearby Golders Green Empire, formerly the largest theatre in London, is now used by BBC Television.

Golders Green crossroads, *c.* 1904. Golders Green probably gets its name from the Goodyere family, local landowners in Tudor times. The tower of the crematorium, opened in 1902, can just be glimpsed in the background.

A total transformation! The memorial to the First and Second World Wars is in the centre and on the left can be seen the railway bridge which carries the underground trains on the Edgware branch of the Northern Line.

The Royal Oak, Temple Fortune on the corner of Bridge Lane looking south in the early 1920s. The exterior staircase of the solid-tyred bus is clearly visible.

Some architectural features of The Royal Oak are still visible but shops built at various times line both sides of the road. The 'Recycling Bank' notice is a modern feature. Citizens are encouraged to take their waste bottles, paper and plastics and put them into special large plastic 'drums' from which they are collected for recycling.

The Mansion, Golders Hill was purchased by Hendon Council from executors of Sir Spencer Wells in 1938 for £338,000.

The Mansion was destroyed in an air raid in 1940. It was replaced by purpose-built refreshment rooms which, although less impressive, continue to cater for the large numbers of visitors to the park.

Hoop Lane, Golders Green was originally Wield Lane, and was renamed after the building of the Hoop public house described, rather kindly, as 'not pretentious'. The first house built in the new suburb of Golders Green was on the corner of Hoop Lane and Finchley Road.

The Golders Green end of Hoop Lane, like so much of the property in this area, was developed with the coming of the underground railway. A few of the original trees have been fortunate enough to survive.

Golders Green Road looking south-east in the late 1920s. The meat carcases hanging outside Messrs Bernards would not pass today's hygiene regulations. Hendon and Finchley Councils both operated electric generating stations. Hendon Council had an office at 43 Golders Green Road. Garments cleaned at the French Cleaning & Dyeing Company would have been delivered by box tricycle. The open-topped no. 83 bus is on its way to Hendon.

Golders Green Road looking north-west. It is a notorious traffic bottleneck made worse by indiscriminate parking. The shops and restaurants are well patronized, although frequent changes of ownership reflect the changes in fashion and lifestyles.

Hermitage Lane, Childs Hill, *c.* 1910. Richard le Childe is mentioned in 1312. The local springs and wells provided water of good quality and in Tudor times the royal washing was done here. The Hermitage was one of several large mansions. Note the complete absence of traffic in this early twentieth-century suburban street. At that time, houses like these were often called 'pretty villas'.

Blocks of flats have replaced the original houses but the road retains some of its spacious characteristics. The left-hand side of the road now features large houses.

Royal Parade, Temple Fortune. The shops here were built to serve the developing community. They are dated 1904 and so must be some of the earliest in the district.

There has been little change to the buildings here but stricter rules now prevent shopkeepers displaying their wares on the pavement. Traffic jams are commonplace on this stretch of road.

Asmuns Place, Hampstead Garden Suburb runs off Hampstead Way. The cottages were designed with Darby and Joan seats near the front doors. The HGS Association was incorporated on 6 March 1906 and the first sod was cut nearby at 140/142 Hampstead Way. The deed of incorporation enabled the purchase of 243 acres of Wylde's Farm. Asmuns is probably a corruption of Ass Man's.

The term 'cottages', as applied to Asmuns Place, is suggestive of the rural atmosphere encouraged by Dame Henrietta Barnett, one of the founders of the Hampstead Garden Suburb Association, and her colleagues. The ubiquitous motor car has spoiled the image.

King George V and Queen Mary visited the Haven of Rest in Homesfield Road on 18 March 1911. There fifty-seven single-room flats were provided for elderly women at cheap rents with separate accommodation nearby for orphaned children. A neat example of Mrs Barnett's intention to provide 'an ideal household with all generations living happily together'.

The idea of orphanages became unfashionable and the Haven of Rest was replaced by modern town houses. It is ironic that what Mrs Barnett intended as houses for the poor from the East End of London have become some of London's most sought-after dwellings.

The original club house on Willifield Green, designed to be a focal point for community activities, was opened in 1910. During the First World War it was used as a military hospital and was itself badly damaged by bombing in 1940.

In 1957, as part of the Garden Suburb's golden jubilee celebrations, the centre was rebuilt to cater for the needs of the over-60s. The very wide range of activities which take place in the hall reflect the many and diverse interests of the local residents.

Dooley's Farm, Mill Hill looking east. Dole is an old word meaning a piece of land. The farm belonged to the Nicoll family, who originated in the fifteenth century, for five generations.

The fields of Dooley's Farm are now the Brookfield housing estate built in 1937.

The almshouses, Milespit Hill looking west. The pond would have been used for watering stock and washing clothes. The almshouses were erected 'at ye year of our Lord 1696 and at the sole charge of Thomas Nicoll'. The white house on the right appears to date from about 1800, although it could be older.

Little has changed here. The almshouses have been modernized and the village pond survives.

Angel Cottages, Milespit Hill, Mill Hill looking north. The origin of Milespit is obscure. Perhaps it comes from Mill Pightle. A pightle is a narrow strip of land. The cottages are timber framed with board cladding possibly dating from the seventeenth century. The Angel pub is shown in the War Office billeting return of 1756 as having accommodation for two horses and two men.

Although Angel Cottages were pulled down in 1964, the new town houses which replaced them retained the old name. The quality and appearance of these houses has been commended in the architectural press and is due in no small measure to the efforts of the Mill Hill Preservation Society who, together with similar pressure groups within the borough, monitor developments and changes and insist on high standards.

The Adam and Eve on the Ridgeway, Mill Hill shortly before it was rebuilt in 1906. Originally called simply The Eve, it was famous for its 'rude' sign. It was also a stopping place in the days of the horse bus. It is said to have been established in 1730, but is not shown under that name in the War Office return of 1756.

The Adam and Eve continues to prosper. The easing of the licensing laws, which permit pubs to remain open most of the day, has been complemented in most cases by the sale of food of a surprisingly high quality.

The Broadway, Mill Hill looking west, *c.* 1930. The first shop built on the Promenade was no. 4, which bore a plaque dated March 1910. The Sacred Heart Church on the left was built in 1923. Its design was heavily influenced by the discovery of Tutankamun's tomb in 1922.

The Catholic church, although relatively modern, ran into severe structural problems and was rebuilt in 1996. The Broadway continues to be a prosperous and busy shopping centre.

Deans Lane, Mill Hill. Street lights are visible so this picture could date from about 1900. Deans Brook rises in Scratchwood and runs past Dean Lane on its way to join the Silk Stream. Yew Tree Farm, also known as Hale Farm, is just visible through the trees. It is said to date back to the fourteenth century.

The John Keble Church, Deans Lane, was named after the leader of the Oxford Movement in the Church of England. The land was bought in 1932, from the site of Holbrook House which was demolished. The church is built on a concrete raft and has an unorthodox square shape designed to permit easy viewing by the congregation. The font is about 250 years old and was reclaimed from Devonshire House, Piccadilly, where it was said to have been used as a corn mortar.

Salvage or Selvage Lane, Mill Hill, *c.* 1925. There was a nearby Selvage Field in 1754. The road is essentially an extension northwards of Deans Lane. It is not clear which name is the older. A sign of the considerable antiquity of the road is the width of the verges showing where cattle widened the road by walking round muddy patches.

Yew Tree Farm in Deans Lane was sold in 1905. The houses seen here were erected after 1929. The gavel used by the Chairman of the Mill Hill Historical Society comes from an oak tree on the site, said to date from 1380.

Hale Cross, Mill Hill. There were two Hales, Upper and Lower, joined by Hale Lane, which is shown on a map of 1597. These weather-boarded buildings might well be hiding timber frames from the Tudor period.

The Green Man pub on the corner of Hale Lane and Selvage Lane is mentioned in the billeting return of 1751, but may be older. At the turn of the twentieth century it was a centre for training boxers and racing greyhounds. This building dates from the late 1920s, when the rest of the estate was developed.

Cricklewood Broadway bustling with life, *c.* 1920. The estate agent was at no. 165 and Highfield laundry at no. 167. The no. 16 bus to Victoria is one of three competing for passengers – a reminder that before the establishment of the London Passenger Transport Board, numbers of private buses vied for passengers along the same routes.

There is little evidence of change to the buildings. The road remains one of the busiest routes to the heart of London and is well served by public transport.

Edgware High Street, The Boot Inn and St Margaret's Church looking east, *c.* 1880. The parish pump is behind the railings on the left. Street lighting has not yet arrived, although the police officer wears the new style of helmet. The road surface is gravelled and shows the marks of cart wheels.

The parish church is still visible behind a row of execrably designed shops whose architecture reflects more the need to build cheaply than add to the attraction of the area.

Stonegrove, Edgware High Street looking north, *c.* 1900. The name probably derives from the nearby ninth milestone from London. Part of Cannons Park is visible on the left. There is a gas street light on the left. The two farm carts on the right have extension pieces for carrying hay, a reminder of the importance of the local crop.

A popular feature of today's life in suburbia is the garden centre, one of which is seen here. They cater for the traditional British love of gardens and countryside. Stonegrove Public Park, just beyond the centre, was opened in 1934.

Edgware High Street from The Chandos Arms, *c.* 1900. There appears to be a water trough outside The George Inn, which was named after the nearby George Farm and not, like so many others, King George.

The old pub has been replaced by shops and flats, a common practice in the 1930s and '50s.

Edgwarebury Lane, *c.* 1930. The name comes from Bury Farm, one of the many places where Dick Turpin is reputed to have stayed.

Shops now dominate both sides of the road. The double-yellow lines, controlling parking, are an indication of the busy nature of this location.

Cannons Park tram terminus looking south, *c.* 1920. There is an AA patrol directing traffic. The first trams ran from Cricklewood to Edgware in 1904 and were extended to Cannons Park in 1907.

A roundabout keeps the traffic flowing at this busy spot now. The old garage with its petrol pumps on the forecourt has been replaced by a typical modern service station where the accent is on self service of fuel and lubricants as well (in some cases) as confectionery, bakery, books, videos and even flowers!

TRANSPORT

Public transport has been vital to the prosperity and survival of most parts of the London Borough of Barnet. Some of the most popular methods of transport used are seen in the following pages.

Long-distance horse buses such as this one, outside The Torrington Arms, Finchley, were in their day a popular method of travel to and from the City and West End. In 1860, for example, about three a day set out and returned to Barnet. The coming of the local railways and trams rendered the horse bus obsolete.

As this photograph taken in about 1911 shows, horses were an essential part of the economy as they had been for centuries. A huge range of carts, traps, gigs and the like were available to meet every commercial and private need.

In the late 1860s and '70s railway companies such as the Great Northern opened lines and branch lines to places such as Edgware and Chipping Barnet, stopping at places such as Mill Hill East, Totteridge, Woodside Park and Finchley Central. The journey from Finchley Central to town, for example, took about half an hour, a workman's fare was 4*d* (in old money) and sixty trains ran daily by 1902. The working classes could at last find jobs outside their immediate locality.

The railways serving the area became part of the Northern Line underground system which was electrified to Edgware and in 1939 to East Finchley and later to Barnet and Mill Hill East. Today, over 30 per cent of daily commuters in the borough do so by underground.

In 1905 a tram service was opened between Highgate and Whetstone which was extended soon after to Chipping Barnet. Other routes were shortly in operation serving such places as Edgware, New Southgate, Golders Green and onwards. Trams were frequent, cheap and an ideal form of transport for intermediate journeys.

It was to be the motor omnibus that finally triumphed in the battle for public road transport. As early as 1908 a bus ran every twelve minutes from North Finchley to Oxford Circus. As this picture shows, these early omnibuses were far from comfortable, particularly for the driver who had no windscreen to protect him. Such buses could also be hired on a daily basis for outings.

The trolleybus was a feature of local routes from about 1936 onwards. They largely replaced the trams and their quietness and speed was an attractive feature. Like the tram, however, they lacked manoeuvrability as the mass of overhead wires in this photograph shows. They were to disappear in about 1959–62 to be replaced by the famous London Transport red buses.

The motor car, at a surprisingly early date, began to make its presence felt on local roads. This charming photograph of a well-known Hadley family and their friends, was taken in about 1910. It reveals some of the joys and convenience of early motoring, although nothing about the notorious mechanical unreliability.